**SEE TO
LEARN**

Remembering C.E.T. (Tim) and
S.C. (Steve) Moss, with love.
— KMG

For Michael, always.
— KP

Lake

A SEE TO LEARN BOOK

Kate Moss Gamblin

Pictures by

Karen Patkau

GROUNDWOOD BOOKS

HOUSE OF ANANSI PRESS

TORONTO   BERKELEY

What do you see when you see a lake?
Do you see, through great pine pillars,
the moving, shimmering water?

Do you see how the wind, ruffling the water and our hair, over time shapes the pine growing at lake's edge?

Do you see all the winged visitors, the dragonfly and hummingbird wings

beating swift enough to hover, swoop and dart?

Do you see the water striders rowing atop the living water, as a school of lake trout swim alongside you and me?

Do you see that countless generations of creatures share the water, its still surface reflecting the ever-changing seasons?

Do you see, under these sheltering willow branches,
the swan and her cygnets, their feathers

lightening through their first autumn, only
their feet busy below?

Do you see this crimson leaf fallen on the water — marker of the turning season — a tiny red canoe on its journey toward the sea?

Do you see the water leaving the lake in silvery tumbles near a bevy of playful otter cubs?

Do you see the morning mist rising to clouds,
as it does above lakes the world over, later
returning as droplets or snow —

snow that feathers all around us?

Do you see a gaggle of curious young goslings, learning to land on firm ice that just yesterday they were able to drink?

Do you see ice protecting life in the heart of
the deep lake until the warm days of spring?

Do you see the season for snowshoes melting away as the tamarack sprouts its springtime coat, the red squirrel finds

its mate, and moose calves wade
through fiddleheads uncurling?

Do you see the trees, dark against the indigo sky, embracing the lake? They stand, quietly at their starlit work, putting the day to bed.

Do you see the lake and trees together,
awaiting the flash of the rising sun?
What do you see when you see a lake?

Author's Note

The See to Learn series points young readers and their adult co-readers toward the wonder of the natural world as an impetus for a deeper relationship with ourselves and our environment. Spending time quietly in nature can reveal the richness of inter-connection between each of us and the many elements around us. Heart solace arises through this sense of connection and of being held in much larger frames than we ordinarily imagine, and is a key aspect of shaping an inner environmental compass.

Direct connection with our natural world is also a gateway to a broader style of perception: our sustainability perspective, moving us beyond our usual spheres of concern about time, place and relationship. There is both a precious transience to time — the single tawny autumn of a cygnet, or that particular stage in a young trout's life as a parr — and an enduring qual-ity, as seen through prevailing winds gradually shaping a pine tree. Possibilities abound for exploring relationships — in tightly defined groups of young animals such as cygnets, goslings or calves, and through the diversity of life included in the collective nouns of school, gaggle and bevy of beings.

Our imaginations are solution innovators, awake in the very young and endlessly available with practice throughout our lives. Our mind's eye helps us perceive different times and places — mist that will later return as rain, or dawn's fresh spark at any given moment on our planet — and guides our everyday choices. Imbued with greater kindness, patience and trust in ourselves and in others, our choices shape our individual and collective future on a planet that is both finite and enough.

Our natural world is a starting point for a conversation about how we share the treasure of our lives to ensure life for all to come, as we See to Learn.

Further Reading

For Young Readers:

All the Water in the World by George Ella Lyon, illustrated by Katherine Tillotson. Atheneum Books for Young Readers, 2011.

Cloudwalker by Roy Henry Vickers and Robert Budd, illustrated by Roy Henry Vickers. Harbour Publishing, 2014.

Loon by Susan Vande Griek, illustrated by Karen Reczuch. Groundwood Books, 2011.

Me and You and the Red Canoe by Jean E. Pendziwol, illustrated by Phil. Groundwood Books, 2017.

Over and Under the Pond by Kate Messner, illustrated by Christopher Silas Neal. Chronicle Books, 2017.

Pond Circle by Betsy Franco, illustrated by Stefano Vitale. Margaret K. McElderry Books, 2009.

Salmon Creek by Annette LeBox, illustrated by Karen Reczuch. Groundwood Books, 2002.

A Walk on the Shoreline by Rebecca Hainnu, illustrated by Qin Leng. Inhabit Media, 2015.

Water Can Be … by Laura Purdie Salas, illustrated by Violeta Dabija. Millbrook Press, 2014.

Water Is Water: A Book About the Water Cycle by Miranda Paul, illustrated by Jason Chin. Roaring Brook Press, 2015.

Groundwood Books / House of Anansi Press
groundwoodbooks.com

We gratefully acknowledge for their financial support of our publishing
program the Canada Council for the Arts, the Ontario Arts Council and
the Government of Canada.

Canada Council   Conseil des Arts
for the Arts   du Canada

ONTARIO ARTS COUNCIL
CONSEIL DES ARTS DE L'ONTARIO
an Ontario government agency
un organisme du gouvernement de l'Ontario

With the participation of the Government of Canada
Avec la participation du gouvernement du Canada | Canadä

Library and Archives Canada Cataloguing in Publication
Title: Lake : a see to learn book / Kate Moss Gamblin ; pictures by Karen Patkau.
Names: Moss Gamblin, Kate, author. | Patkau, Karen, illustrator.
Series: Moss Gamblin, Kate. See to learn.
Description: Series statement: See to learn
Identifiers: Canadiana (print) 20190227621 | Canadiana (ebook) 20190227656 |
ISBN 9781554988815 (hardcover) | ISBN 9781554988822 (EPUB) |
ISBN 9781773064284 (Kindle)
Subjects: LCSH: Lake ecology—Juvenile literature. |
LCSH: Lakes—Juvenile literature.
Classification: LCC QH541.5.L3 M67 2020 | DDC j577.63—dc23

The artwork in *Lake: A See to Learn Book* was digitally rendered.
Design by Michael Solomon
Printed and bound in China

MIX
Paper from
responsible sources
FSC® C144853
FSC
www.fsc.org